THE
ENCOURAGEMENT
FACTOR

How to Radically Transform Your Relationship in 14 Days

BIBLE STUDY & ACTION PLAN
KIRK POSER

Ten|16
PRESS

www.ten16press.com - Waukesha, WI

The Encouragement Factor: How to Radically Transform
Your Relationship in 14 Days
Copyright © 2022 by Kirk Poser
9781645384472
First Edition

The Encouragement Factor How to Radically Transform Your
Relationship in 14 Days
by Kirk Poser

For information, please contact:

Ten|16
PRESS

www.ten16press.com
Waukesha, WI

Editor: Pam Parker
Cover Designer: Kaeley Dunteman

Advanced praise for

THE ENCOURAGEMENT FACTOR

"The timing of this new book could not be better; the need for encouragement is greater than ever. I love how [Kirk Poser] explains that encouragement 'makes life easier for people.' What a beautiful idea."

-Ben Davis, Lead Pastor at RiverGlen Christian Church

"[This book] was easy to read, actionable, and clear. I'm excited for the outcome!"

-Tabatha Frozena, Sales Director at Concurrency

"Uplifting, optimistic, and easy to read. Kirk's message reminds us all of the importance of maintaining good communication with those we are close to, and that we must always be sure to encourage and be encouraged by those we love. Regardless of one's faith or circumstances, a kind word in the right place can mean all the difference in the world."

-William Purdy, Studio Director at Spectrum Fusion Studios

"[Kirk] builds a strong case for people to become deliberate encouragers. We live in a time where we are surrounded by discouragement. Turn on the news, pick up a paper, or click on social media, and you will be bombarded with turmoil and discontentment.

Words matter. Spoken words are the outpouring of an inner thought's life. To be an encourager is to be one who lets go of the discouragement around us and focuses on the good in others and in our world. An encourager adds life to all. In the process of encouraging, it's not only the recipient who changes. The encourager, themself, is impacted through the process.

Luke 6:45, in effect, says, the mouth speaks from the outpouring of the heart. To encourage, is to be encouraged. Just as it is better to give than to receive, it is better to encourage than to be encouraged. Everyone gains when this system is employed."

-John Howard, Care Ministry & Waukesha Outreach Lead

"This quick-read reference should not be underestimated. The examples in [this book] are so inspiring—the reminder that through individual encouragement, we can also change the world. The ripple effect, the impact that a single gesture can have, is so perfectly illustrated in these pages.

I love the poignant biblical references, connecting Christ's love for us to the love we desire to show our partner. I particularly was intrigued and inspired by the suggestions regarding what men need versus women. As a woman, feeling that security, love, appreciation, and safety—all are so important to my core and my soul. The understanding that men have an innate desire to feel not just loved, but also respected, is so powerful as I start this journey with my own partner.

The power of encouragement is something that indeed is life-changing, not only for the receiver but also for the giver. I have already started my journey using *The Encouragement Factor* and can't wait to share my own experience.

Knowing [Kirk] as my friend for so many years, I loved reading this and at the same time heard his voice in every word. His careful, kind, and thoughtful delivery comes through beautifully in the message."

-Kate Weiland, Chief Operations Officer for Concurrency, Inc.

DEDICATION

I would like to dedicate this book first to my wife, Susan. She has taught me so many things in our life together: to be generous, to be thoughtful, to be an encourager. She is my biggest fan.

Second, to all the people who have used the methodology and shared their feedback with me. Seeing lives change is a dream for me that came to life in this book.

Lastly, my thanks where it needs to go foremost: to God who provided me with the gifts to write and share this methodology to work for His glory in the Kingdom! If this book changes your life, I want to hear about it! Reach me at kaptinkirk@msn.com

THE ENCOURAGEMENT FACTOR

Our world is difficult to navigate, more now than ever as events happening around us make us uneasy and sometimes simply afraid.

Throughout history, we have always looked for ways to cope with life's ups and downs. Sometimes those ways come from alcohol or other drugs. Sometimes we don't cope at all and retreat or withdraw.

As humans we all have basic needs: food, water, air. These basic needs keep the machine we call our body functioning.

But what does our soul need?

This book will take you on a journey. Use it as a guidepost on making an impact in this world. Sometimes you will see immediate results, other times it may not become known to you until much later.

But you will know.

GOD CAN DO AMAZING THINGS WHEN HE IS INVITED INTO THE SMALL DETAILS OF YOUR LIFE. HE WILL HELP YOU ENCOURAGE OTHERS IF YOU LET HIM.

CHAPTER 1

HOW DO I USE THIS BOOK?

If you are a Christian, you most likely have done a study or two in your spiritual journey.

Think of this as a different type of study, one with an action plan. Follow the plan and you will impact a relationship of your choice. In return, those actions will impact you in an amazing way.

You can choose to do this study independently or in a group setting. Either application will work well.

WHAT IF I AM NOT A CHRISTIAN?

Don't worry, this book will still be of immense value to you. The principles and methodology are the same. Completing the study and actions won't bring faith to you, but they might bring you to faith when you see the results.

Hopefully through this book, you will begin to see the purpose God has for you in this life, and it will cause you to find out more. I hope so!

WHAT ARE THE MOST IMPORTANT TRUTHS YOU WILL LEARN?

People (especially men) struggle to
compliment our spouses enough.

People need to hear encouraging words
from others to help navigate life.

People need an easy way to share what they feel.

ARE THERE ANY DISCLAIMERS?

This process is not a one and done; rather, this is
an investment into the life of another person or persons. Rebuilding or creating a relationship with another person requires a time commitment. Your time
and energy are needed to make positive changes.

ANY GUARANTEES?

This will either change your life, the life of another person, or both. You have my word. No gimmicks, no tricks. Just some life-changing things going down.

I know you can do this. You've got this because
you have been fearfully and wonderfully made!

ARE YOU READY TO IMPLEMENT A CHANGE IN YOUR LIFE?

LET'S DO IT!

CHAPTER 2

Why do we need encouragement?

Look around you…what do you see?

I see people struggling to make ends meet. I see people in crisis as their marriage crumbles around their family. I see people bearing enormous levels of grief and pain. I see children faltering in school.

I see a world that needs help. Don't you? Don't we all? I believe increasing the number of encouragers among us could help.

So, what does it really mean to encourage someone?

Encouragement is a heart tonic. The word "encourage" comes from a combination of the prefix en- which means "to put into" and the Latin root cor which means "heart".

If you are alive, you need encouragement! As human beings, we were created with a strong desire and need for encouragement. I believe we are wired that way from our Creator!

> *"Therefore encourage one another and build each other up, just as in fact you are doing."*
> 1 Thessalonians 5:11

> *"May the God who gives endurance and encouragement give you the same attitude of mind toward each other that Christ Jesus had..."*
> Romans 15:5

An encouraging word spoken at the right time can make all the difference in a person's life. I have friends for whom in the middle of a struggle, a simple "You got this" or "You are really good at this" have initiated a complete turnaround of attitude from negative to positive. Later in the book we will walk through the methodology of how encouraging words can work, and you will have a better understanding on how sometimes a simple word of encouragement will change your relationship. Jill, one of the many people who have used what you will learn shared this: "Simple, handwritten notes of appreciation, thoughtfulness and encouragement were tucked away in places that my eyes would fall upon them just when I needed it most! In the busyness of life with three boys and full-time work, this gesture kept my heart entwined with my husband's!"

> Scripture says in Proverbs 25:11, *"The right word at the right time is like precious gold set in silver."*

How can words change the course of one's life? Here we find the paradox. We are wired with the need to receive encouragement, yet it isn't natural for most of us to deliver it.

ESPECIALLY men.

As believers, our faith teaches us that this life is temporal, we are simply passing through. I believe this with all my heart. But as we are passing through, God has impressed certain things on our hearts that he wishes us to accomplish on this earth first. Think of these wishes as your good works.

Sharing good works or deeds—expecting nothing in return—will not seal the deal to a greater reward, Jesus does. But if you truly are following Jesus, good works should come out of you as easily as air. (Well maybe not that easily, but it shouldn't be hard.) If you are a non-believer, good works are good deeds or doing something for someone without expecting anything in return. Remember how good you felt lending someone a hand and feeling appreciated?

SO, BACK TO WHY WE NEED ENCOURAGEMENT.

1. Encouragement will help change the world.

We lament daily that something must change. We look to others to fix the world, make it right. Make me happy again. What if fixing the world really was simple, but just took effort? Would you do it?

Encouraging someone has a ripple effect. I am sure you have heard this illustration before. You throw a rock into a lake and watch the ripples (rings) spread out from that one single motion. Now imagine multiple ripples intersecting each other. Your encouraging ripples are impacting the world around you. And after all, isn't that your world – the one you interact with? When positively influencing those around you, you may never know how they in turn spread encouragement to someone else. But that's okay. Trust that these positives multiply and spread.

2. It may very well change someone's life (possibly their eternity).

Sometimes a person only needs a little boost, a helping hand, a kind word. Any one of these actions can change a person's outlook at that instant, which could impact their day and how they treat themselves or others. Remember that ripple effect? Touching one person's perspective could impact multiple people, who impact multiple people and so on. Always wanted a superpower? Here you go!

3. You will cultivate relationships.

One of the side benefits of encouraging someone else is you will develop friendships. I believe every good thing returns another good thing. Not in like value perhaps, but in many ways that are hard to explain. Maybe your heart softens a little, maybe you just feel good, who knows? Encouraging others will encourage you, trust me.

4. You will feel good.

Did you ever pay attention to the warm feeling you have when you help someone? The small smile that comes upon your face after doing something good. That little skip in your step, that feeling that is hard to explain. Why does giving something away feel so good?

- ♥ Words Of Affirmation
- ♥ Quality Time
- ♥ Receiving Gifts
- ♥ Acts Of Service
- ♥ Physical Touch

CHAPTER 3

Want to really be an Encourager?

1. Learn people's "love languages," the special ways they communicate and understand love. In his book, The Five Love Languages, Gary Chapman explains that not everyone's emotional needs are met in the same way, and that it's important to learn to adapt ourselves to their needs. According to Chapman, the five love languages are: words of affirmation, quality time, receiving gifts, acts of service, and physical touch.

2. Encourage others often and make sure your words are sincere.

3. When you introduce someone, or your spouse, add a few words of sincere praise for their abilities and accomplishments. People are encouraged to hear praise in front of others.

4. Sending flowers is an amazing pick-me-up. Flowers show you are thinking of them, enough to spur action to send flowers, one of those great ways to let someone know that they are important to you. Think about other things you can send. In this book we are focused on the Post-it note methodology, but actually sending a note in the mail could be an incredible way of encouraging and sharing love. Send something every few days in the mail. Something for that person to look forward to. Life changing! Snail mail that matters is rare these days.

5. Ask people if you could pray for them when they share something that isn't going well in their life, then DO IT! On the spot, say a prayer. It doesn't need to be eloquent, but to pray out loud at that very moment shares that you BELIEVE in the power of prayer and want to share it with them.

6. Celebrate victories. Make it special regardless of if they are large or small. Maybe a coffee together, a special meal, a text or phone call, or just a high-five! Make it clear that they are special!

7. Be specific when you offer words of praise; it makes your encouragement more credible: "You did a great job at...", "I really appreciate that you...", "I was really impressed when you..."

8. Just realizing how valuable it is to be there for a person can in return be encouraging for you!

9. If you're part of a church, a Bible study, a group of coffee aficionados, or simply a group that likes to hang out, show up purposefully. Your consistent presence encourages others that they are part of a community and they are not alone. As part of your community, whatever that looks like, you are in a unique position to impact someone's life with encouragement. That's why the writer of Hebrews says, "Let us not give up the habit of meeting together, as some are in the habit of doing, but let us encourage one another-and all the more as we see the Day approaching." Hebrews 10:25

10. Use encouragement as a form of outreach. If anyone should be known for being an encourager, it should be Christians. I am not saying this is unique to Christians, everyone should be doing this. If you are a follower of Jesus, leading by example will strengthen your conviction to love people. Write a letter of appreciation to people at work, your apartment manager, your child's teacher, or your doctor. Often when we interact with these people, we are asking for their services. Please remember to thank them.

WHAT DOES THE BIBLE SAY ABOUT ENCOURAGEMENT?

CHAPTER 4

A 6-week study in encouragement

Has anyone ever come up to you and said, "Nice work," or, "Good Job!" How did that feel? Have you ever helped someone yourself and felt that warm happiness that seems to fill your being?

Our world needs encouragement now more than ever! SO...

What does the bible say about encouragement?

Let's spend some time together researching, contemplating, and maybe even journaling about this question. This study will focus on the New Testament but will also draw wisdom from the Old Testament or Hebrew Bible too. When you read the bible verse, go into your bible, and read a section or two before and after to understand the complete context of what I chose to focus on.

WEEK 1

Read Hebrews 3:13
"But encourage one another daily, as long as it is called Today, so that none of you may be hardened by sin's deceitfulness."

What thoughts first come to mind when reading this scripture? What three points are made in this scripture and why do you think they are important? The purpose of these questions is to draw people back to the bible or introduce them to the bible. Read the context of the verses before and after, and meditate on the content. They may not be easy questions to answer. The concept of "Today" could refer to the idea of "as long as you are alive."

Why do you think the scripture includes the wording "as long as it is called Today"? Could this also refer to (while you still can?)

From a relationship perspective, share what happens in your relationship when one or both of you get mad. Are you still mad long after it is called today?

Let's go back and expand the context a little and read the verse before our verse:

> "See to it, brothers and sisters that none of you has a sinful, unbelieving heart that turns away from the living God. But encourage one another daily, as long as it is called Today, so that none of you may be hardened by sin's deceitfulness" (Hebrews 3:12-13)

Does this added context change your initial thoughts? How so?

How do you think we are being deceived when the scripture refers to "hardened by sin's deceitfulness"?

How might you encourage someone, so they don't become "hardened by sin's deceitfulness"? What ideas come to mind?

Homework: Develop a list of people close to you, with whom you have a relationship, especially consider folks who might need encouragement. Start with your family, then add in some friends. Not just any friend right now, someone close. We will expand upon this list in future weeks.

WEEK 2

Read 1 Thessalonians 5:11
"Therefore encourage one another and build each other up, just as in fact you are doing."

What thoughts first come to mind when reading this scripture?

_____

_____

_____

Do you think "to encourage" and to "build each other up" are two different concepts?

_____

_____

_____

Who is "one another"?

_____

_____

_____

Write down an example of someone you encouraged lately. What did you do? Did this help that person? How? How did you feel about it?

_____

_____

_____

_____

Throughout the Bible we see instructions to encourage one another and verses that are meant to encourage us. Why do you think encouragement is emphasized so many times in the Bible?

_____

_____

_____

_____

WEEK 3

Read John 16:33

"Jesus told His followers, 'In this world you will have trouble. But take heart! I have overcome the world.'"

What does this verse tell us about the world we live in? Did you become a Christian thinking your world would become easier? Discuss why you think it may become more difficult. If, as a non-believer, you are struggling with this world or your circumstances, does this provide an alternative perspective on how to approach what life throws at you?

_____

_____

_____

Does this verse reassure you at all? How do you feel?

Without encouragement in our world, hardship becomes difficult, and our will to go on fades. The prophet Elijah struggled with discouragement, so we are not alone.

_____

_____

_____

Read 1 Kings 19:3-10

"Elijah was afraid and fled for his life. He went to Beersheba, a town in Judah, and he left his servant there. 4 Then he went on alone into the wilderness, traveling all day. He sat down under a solitary broom tree and prayed that he might die. 'I have had enough, LORD," he said. 'Take my life, for I am no better than my ancestors who have already died."'

Do you know someone in your *sphere of influence who is discouraged? What are they struggling with? *Sphere of influence in this context is someone you already have a trusting relationship with.

What steps can you take to encourage them? List out a few ideas.

_____

_____

_____

_____

Homework: Remember in Week 1, we started to compose a list of people within our sphere of influence who need encouragement? Your homework now is to pray daily for the people on this list. Ask God to help them in their struggle, and how he might want you to encourage them. Journal during this process.

Reference Page 15

WEEK 4

This world overflows with struggles: financial, emotional, and internal. Some people are good at dealing with struggles, some are not. You will never know which one you are until you are in the middle of it.

> Read Acts 4:36
> *"For instance, there was Joseph, the one the apostles nicknamed Barnabas (which means 'Son of Encouragement'). He was from the tribe of Levi and came from the island of Cyprus."*

Barnabas was a huge encouragement to the believers of his day! Thanks to Barnabas, the apostle Paul was first accepted by the church in Jerusalem.

Is there anyone in your life that you might nickname Barnabas?

_____

What makes that person stand out to be worthy of such a title?

_____

_____

_____

_____

What steps can you take today to work towards becoming a Barnabas?

_____

_____

_____

_____

> ### Read Acts 9:27
> "*Then Barnabas brought him to the apostles and told them how Saul had seen the Lord on the way to Damascus and how the Lord had spoken to Saul. He also told them that Saul had preached boldly in the name of Jesus in Damascus.*"

How did Barnabas encourage Saul?

Relationship tip: Praise someone in front of others. It will literally DOUBLE the impact.

_____

_____

_____

_____

WEEK 5

Encouragement makes it easier to live in a fallen world. Encouragement will impact a person to feel what it is like to be loved as Jesus loved.

> ### Read John 13:34-35
> "*So now I am giving you a new commandment: Love each other. Just as I have loved you, you should love each other. Your love for one another will prove to the world that you are my disciples.*"

Encouragement shows us what hope looks like.
Are hope and encouragement connected?

> Read Romans 15:4
> *"Such things were written in the Scriptures long ago to teach us. And the Scriptures give us hope and encouragement as we wait patiently for God's promises to be fulfilled."*

How do you think encouragement and love work together?

_____

_____

_____

What words come to mind that are the opposite of the word "hope"?

_____

_____

_____

_____

In your own words, define what "hope" means to you personally.
How might you share words of hope with someone?

_____

_____

_____

_____

WEEK 6

Encouragement nurtures patience and kindness.

> ### Read 1 Corinthians 13:4-7
> *"Love is patient and kind; love does not envy or boast; it is not arrogant or rude. It does not insist on its own way; it is not irritable or resentful; it does not rejoice at wrongdoing but rejoices with the truth. Love bears all things, believes all things, hopes all things, endures all things."*

Why would patience and kindness need to be part of encouraging someone?

_____

_____

_____

Encouragement makes it easier to put our desires as secondary as compared to the advancement of God's kingdom. Encouragement will make it easier to live the Christian life. When you hear the words "Take up the cross," it means to die to oneself. If you haven't started or are early in your Spiritual Journey, this may make no sense to you. Essentially, it means that when you position yourself to elevate others before your own self-interests, you have "died to self."

> Read John 15:13
> *"Greater love has no one than this: to lay down one's life for one's friends."*

What does it mean to you to "Take up the cross"? Be specific.

_____

_____

Without encouragement, life can feel pointless and troublesome. Without encouragement, we can be over-whelmed by the very real pains of our lives. Without encouragement, we can feel unloved.

Without encouragement, we can easily feel that God doesn't really care about us. Without encouragement, we can lose hope. Hope isn't just for Christians; it is meant for everyone. And God does care, but you may not understand that yet. Read John 3:16, a loving description of how much God does care for ALL people!

So, we need to encourage one another, to remind each other of the truth that God loves us, that God equips us, that we are treasured, that our struggles are worth it.

> Read Proverbs 16:24
> *"Pleasant words are a honeycomb, sweet to the soul and healing to the bones."*

All throughout the bible, God's Word is full of encouragement.

Do you truly understand how powerful words are? Explain in your own words what you believe about the power of words.

If Jesus is the Word, what does this say about his power?

_____

_____

_____

THE GIFT OF ENCOURAGEMENT

The gift of encouragement or exhortation is found in Paul's list of gifts. (Maybe we need a statement earlier about how the study will predominantly focus on the New Testament, with a few sections from the Hebrew Bible and an explanation why and re how non-believers will benefit too?

Read Romans 12:7-8

The word translated "encouragement" or "exhortation" is the Greek word paraklésis, which is related to the word paraclete. Paraklésis basically means "a call to one's side."

Paraklésis carries the idea of bringing someone closely alongside so you can urge, encourage, give joy, and comfort him or her.'

All of these actions fall under the gift of encouragement.

On the night of Jesus being arrested in the garden, Jesus spoke of the Holy Spirit as the "Helper" or "Comforter."

Read John 14:16, 26; 15:26

This is why the Holy Spirit is sometimes referred to as the "Paraclete," the One who comes alongside to encourage us. What spiritual gifts do you think you have? Are you an encourager?

_____

_____

_____

Have you used your gifts for God's purpose lately? How or why not?

_____

_____

Encouragement is useful in counseling, discipleship, mentoring, and preaching. The body of Christ is built up in faith with the gift of encouragement.

When was the last time you sent an encouraging note to your Pastor or the Church staff? What did you write? Was it encouraging or was it about something you didn't like? If you don't belong to a faith community, consider the other organizations you do belong to. Surely there are leaders and active participants who would appreciate some encouragement.

Who else in your life needs encouraging? Your children? Your parents? Your boss?

_____

_____

_____

_____

When was the last time you sent an encouraging note or spoke encouraging words to them?

_____

_____

_____

Write a plan on how you might do this before the week's end.

_____

_____

_____

Encouraging someone, encouraging everyone, is food for the soul, yours and the person receiving it.

Below are 8 steps to be an encourager, or become a better one. In your group, discuss each step and what it means to you. Can you come up with more steps?

THE 8 STEPS OF AN ENCOURAGER

1. Listen before you encourage, to understand where they need "specific" encouragement.

2. Invest time in the person needing encouragement.

3. Ask permission to share a story about how you or someone you know went through the same thing.

4. Ask more or deeper questions to better understand where they may need encouragement.

5. Ask to pray for them and pray over what you heard they needed.

6. Stay connected. Encouragement isn't one and done.

7. Think of ways you can brighten their life and lift them up.

8. Pray to God for ways to show the love of Jesus to this person.

What from the above could you do a better job with?

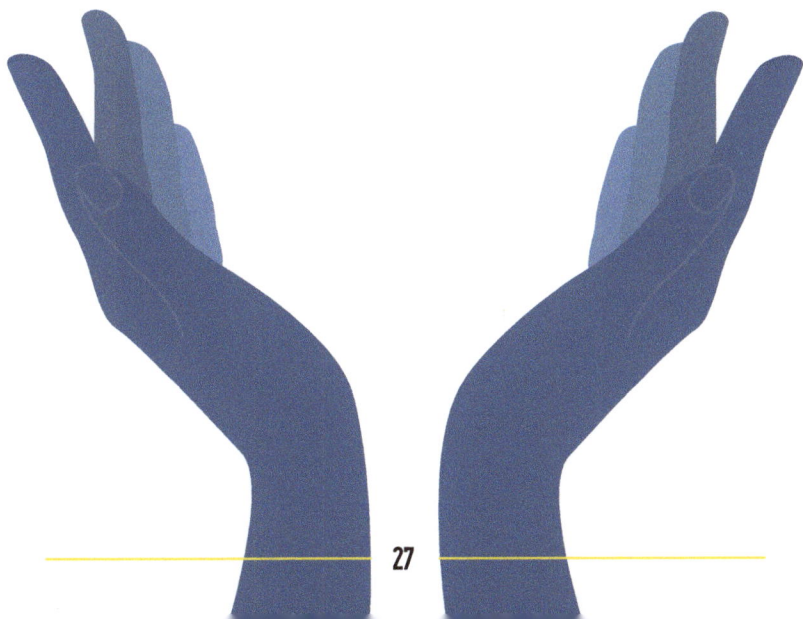

CHAPTER 5

The Man Methodology (Secret sauce)

This program may seem easy on the surface, almost too simplistic. In fact, it is so simple that anyone, any age, can do it. Let me assure you this will not be as easy as it sounds. Remember, this process isn't natural for us.

Let me lay out the program, then we can talk about how it might fail. The methodology won't fail, but you might fail the methodology. Don't worry too much about a failure, we can easily course-correct with minimal impact. We will return to this shortly.

The process I am about to share is a series of steps over 14 days. Not 13 days, not when you feel like it, 14 consecutive days. This is a LOT harder than the ask sounds, so keep that in mind for the next 14 days.

Here we go.

Let's start with the Men first and how following this methodology has saved countless relationships, and successfully enhanced marriages. And let's start out from a man's perspective. Why? This program will be harder for men than women, trust me.

Let's assume a husband is planning to work the program for his wife, for their marriage. The scenario could look something like this: You have been married about 5 years, maybe have your first child, an important, but stressful job, and things get hard just doing life. The responsibility weighs heavy on you. You are starting to lose connection with your wife.

Time to take action!

DAY 1

Step 1: Get yourself a pad of Post-it Notes. It doesn't matter what color or if they have lines or not. Buy the larger version if you can't write small to make the words fit.

Step 2: Find a few quiet moments alone, write on the Post-it note what you love most about your spouse. Remember, you are taking on the challenge of being an encourager, so take this seriously.

Here is an example of a good one to start with, and feel free to use it to get started. It's simple and has proven an easy way to start.

HONEY, I KNOW I DON'T SAY THIS ENOUGH, BUT YOU ARE AN AMAZING MOM!

Step 3: Discreetly stick this somewhere your spouse will find it easily. IMPORTANT: Do not tell them you are doing anything, don't draw attention to it, just put it somewhere easy, after all this is day 1. Now just wait. She may or not say anything when she finds it. Don't be discouraged if she simply thinks that this is a nice gesture, and it makes her feel good.

Step 4: When she finds it, if you happen to be close by, watch her reaction…her smile and her body language. If she asks anything about what you are doing, simply say something like: "just thought you needed to hear this today."

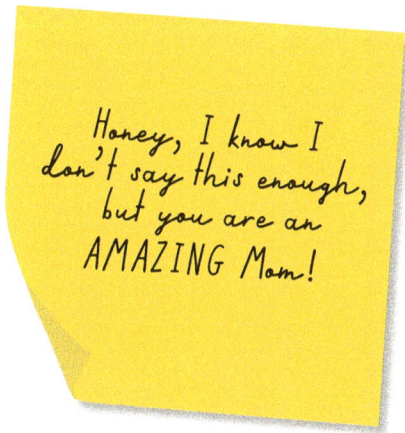

Honey, I know I don't say this enough, but you are an AMAZING Mom!

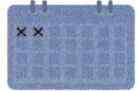

DAY 2

Step 5: Time for another Post-it note. I have found this works best at night before going to bed, or early in the morning, depending on when you have time to think. Same thing as Day 1 but find another "easy" place where you know she will easily find it. Spend some quiet time thinking about what to write. Go back in time and think about what attracted you to her, or whatever comes to mind, and write it down. Be SINCERE. And when she finds it, don't say anything about it. Talking about this will come later

YOU AMAZE ME HOW WELL YOU KEEP THIS HOUSE TOGETHER, EVEN WHEN I SOMETIMES MESS THINGS UP - THANK YOU!

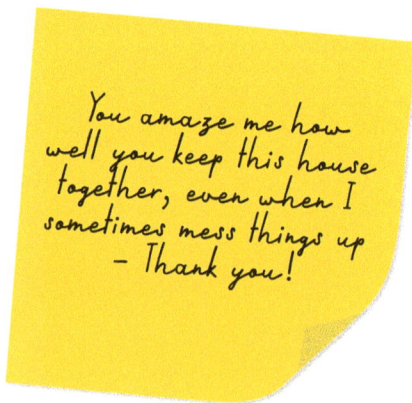

You amaze me how well you keep this house together, even when I sometimes mess things up – Thank you!

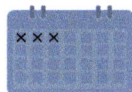

DAY 3

Step 6: Same as step 5. Make sure to put the notes in places that are easy to find the first couple of days, but not the same exact location each day. Don't be afraid of someone else in the family seeing the notes. Remember, we lead by example.

Step 7: Same as step 6 with some caveats.

HERE IS WHAT CAN GO WRONG: The first few days are easy but here is where life can trip you up.

Don't miss a day.

Three days "should be easy" but from here forward it is critical that you do not break the pattern. Not even a single day. This is a proven methodology, don't try to change things right now. Stick with the plan.

DAY 4

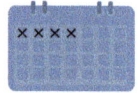

Step 8: Today is day 4, and it is probably not as easy as the first three days to come up with something to write. Take your time. Find a quiet spot and think. You may find it difficult to focus for long but do your best. Starting today, put the Post-it notes in a little harder place to find, but don't make them search for it (yet). Some good examples might be: the refrigerator, your wife's car dashboard, the treadmill, or her purse. The key is she still needs to find it daily, so don't make it too hard! Have fun with this!

DAY 5

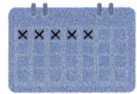

Step 9: From today going forward, it may become harder to come up with those specific, encouraging thoughts to write, but more fun to hide (and find). Allow extra time to write as it's getting more difficult to think of what to write. Get creative in your placement locations. Maybe in her Day-Timer, or in her car on the dashboard. Somewhere you know she will find it that day, but let it be fun. Just as you can't miss a day writing it, they can't either if they can't find it.

DAY 6

Note: By the time you get to day 6 or sooner, she will be anxiously waiting to see what pops up next and where. You will see her in a different light as each day goes on. You may even hear her telling one of her friends what is going on and how fun it is.

DAY 7 FORWARD TO DAY 14

Step 10: Continue to Day 14. Do not miss a day, and don't get lazy in your written notes. It can get easier to write something that won't encourage here because it will get harder every day. It can be helpful sometimes to just ask yourself: what's one thing she did yesterday that I noticed and appreciated? Think about observing her interacting with another family member. Did she handle a difficult situation with grace?

DAY 15

She will miss the fun of the daily routine, but will be so full of encouragement, she will be overflowing knowing she is loved and how she is loved by YOU.

Bonus: You will find you have also benefited from this. You have just reminded yourself of fourteen different reasons why you fell in love. Fourteen times your hearts have been touched with love, and you both will be filled up with a rekindled fire you haven't felt in perhaps quite some time.

NOW is the time to find a babysitter, book a getaway even if it is just for one night, and take your "bride" away for a night that will feel even better than a honeymoon. **You can thank me later!**

Note: After fourteen days, the work is done, and most likely you have been reaping the benefits: a recharged relationship, rekindled fire you perhaps haven't felt for quite some time, or perhaps just a general sense of happiness and joy. I don't recommend continuing after 14 days, because then it may become a chore and not have the impact we are looking for. Can you do this again a few months down the road, or maybe next year? ABSOLUTELY! You can truly never encourage someone too much!

CHAPTER 6

Samples for Men to use with their spouse or significant other

To many, this exercise will not be easy, but please don't get discouraged. Find a quiet spot to sit and think. To help spur you on, here are some sample notes/messages to refer to. There is no shame in using these!

If you are married:

1. Honey, there is no doubt in my mind that I love you more today than when we got married.

2. The way you keep the family schedule together is a feat most people can't even come close to.

3. I love waking up next to you in the morning. It causes me to smile and thank God for you in my life.

4. I pray for our marriage every morning when I wake up, as I never want anything to come between us.

If you are with a significant other:

1. I can't wait for the day we can become husband and wife.

2. Meeting you has been a blessing from God for me, thanks for coming into my life.

3. Did you ever think we could be so happy together? This is amazing!

4. Doing life with you is such fun, you are such a giving person, and I am learning so much!

Get creative, get playful!
If you love seeing your wife in the shower, let her know that. You need to be her biggest fan, always!

I can't wait for the day we can become husband and wife.

CHAPTER 7

The Woman Methodology (Secret sauce)

This program may seem easy on the surface, almost too simplistic. In fact, it is so simple, anyone, any age can do it. Let me assure you this will not be as easy as it sounds. Remember, this isn't natural for us.

Let me lay out the program, then we can talk about how this can fail. The methodology won't fail, but you could fail the methodology. We will return to this shortly.

The process I am about to share is a series of steps over fourteen days. Not thirteen days, not when you feel like it, fourteen consecutive days. This is a LOT harder than the ask sounds, so keep that in mind for the next fourteen days.

What do you think about a little calendar illustration here with days marked off or highlighted?

Here we go.

Let's start with the process that has saved relationships and successfully enhanced marriages. And let's look at this process from a woman's perspective. Why? In my experience with previous groups and individuals, this process will be much easier for women than men, but not in all aspects.

Note: If you haven't heard this before, women need to know they are loved; men need to know they are respected. Our needs create a critical BIG difference!

Let's talk about that idea a little. Women are emotional creatures. Loving, caring, nurturing creations of God. Men, for the most part, not so much. That's not to say that men don't love, care or nurture, but it's not our greatest strength. So, when you want to convey a message of love to your husband, he needs to hear it in words that show respect. He loves to hear you say that you love him, but he needs to hear it in words that convey trust and admiration. He needs to know he is doing things right, and that you look up to him as a leader, in the family, the church, the world. The thing about men is that if you plant the right seed, and nurture it to grow, your husband can rise to do amazing things!

So, what does that look like? The scenario may look something like this: You have been married about five years, maybe have your first child, you might be a stay-at-home mom or hold a high-pressure career job. Regardless of career direction, you are tired, and filling up your husband's love tank is the farthest thing from your mind. You are starting to lose connection with your husband.

Time to take action!

DAY 1

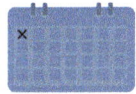

Step 1: Get yourself a pad of sticky notes. It doesn't matter what color or if they have lines or not. Buy the larger version if you can't write small to make the words fit.

Step 2: Find a few quiet moments alone, and write on the note what you love most about your spouse. Remember, you are taking on the challenge of being an encourager, so take this seriously.

How do I convey respect to my husband?
Here is an example of a good one to start with and feel free to use it to get started. It has proven simple and an easy way to start.

HONEY, I KNOW I DON'T SAY THIS ENOUGH, BUT YOU ARE AN AMAZING DAD OR HUSBAND!

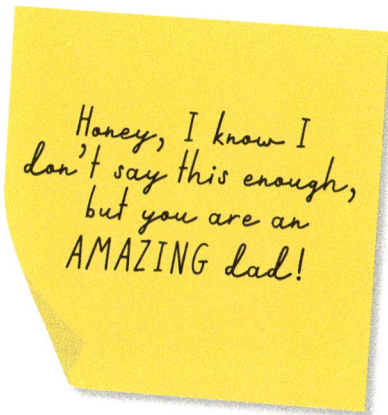

Honey, I know I
don't say this enough,
but you are an
AMAZING dad!

Step 3: Stick this discreetly somewhere where your spouse will find it easily. IMPORTANT: Do not tell them you are doing anything, don't draw attention to it, just put it somewhere easy to find, after all this is day 1. Now just wait. He may or not say anything when he finds it. Don't be discouraged if he simply thinks that this is a nice gesture, and it makes him feel good.

Step 4: When he finds it, if you happen to be close by, watch his reaction…his smile and his body language. If he asks anything about what you are doing, simply say something like: "just thought you needed to hear this today."

DAY 2

Step 5: Time for another note. I have found that this works the best at night before going to bed, or early in the morning depending on when you have time to think. Same thing as Day 1 but find another place where you know he will easily find it. Spend some quiet time thinking about what to write. Go back in time and think about what attracted you to him, or whatever comes to mind, and write it down. Be SINCERE. And when he finds it, don't say anything about it. Talking about this will come later.

HONEY, THE WAY YOU MANAGE OUR FINANCES MAKES ME FEEL SAFE THAT YOU LEAD THIS FAMILY.

Honey, The way you manage our finances makes me feel safe that you lead this family.

DAY 3

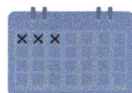

Step 6: Same as step 5. Make sure the notes are placed in easy to find locations for the first couple of days, but not the same location each day. Don't be afraid of someone else in the family seeing the notes. Remember, we lead by example.

Step 7: Same as step 6 with some caveats.

HERE IS WHAT CAN GO WRONG: The first few days are easy but here is where life can trip you up.

Don't miss a day.

Three days "should be easy", but from here forward it is critical that you do not break the pattern. Not even a single day. This is a proven methodology; don't try to change the plan.

DAY 4

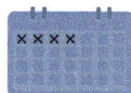

Step 8: Today is day 4, and it is probably not as easy as the first three days to come up with something to write. Take your time. Find a quiet spot and think. You may find it very difficult to focus for long but do the best you can. Starting today, start putting the Post-it notes in a little harder place to find, but don't make them search for it (yet). Some examples: In his Day-Timer (if he uses such a thing) or on his To Do list. Does he take a lunch bag? Hide it there. How about inside his car somewhere – dashboard or inside on the windshield? Get creative.

DAY 5

Step 9: From today going forward, it will likely become harder to write the notes, but more fun to hide (and find). Allow extra time to write as it's getting more difficult to think about what to write. Get creative in your placement locations. Maybe tucked in his wallet or his toolbox. Somewhere you know he will find it that day, but let it be fun. Just as you can't miss a day writing it, he can't either if he can't find it.

DAY 6

Note: By the time you get to day 6 or sooner, he will be anxiously waiting to see what pops up next and where. You will see him in a different light as each day goes on. You may even hear him telling one of his buddies what is going on and how fun it is.

DAY 7 THROUGH DAY 14

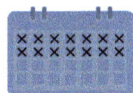

Step 10: Continue to Day 14. Do not miss a day and don't get lazy in your writings. It can be tempting to write something that won't encourage him because it will get harder every day.

DAY 15

He will miss the fun of the daily routine, but will be so full of encouragement, he will be overflowing knowing he is loved and most importantly RESPECTED and how he is loved by YOU.

BONUS: You will find you have also benefited from this. You have just reminded yourself fourteen different ways why you fell in love. Fourteen times your heart has been touched with love, and you will be filled up with a re-kindled fire you haven't felt in perhaps quite some time.

NOW is the time to find a babysitter, book a getaway even if it is just for one night, and take your "Groom" away for a night that will feel even better than a honeymoon. **You can thank me later!**

Note: After fourteen days, the work is done, and most likely you have been reaping the benefits: a recharged relationship, a rekindled fire you perhaps haven't felt for quite some time, or maybe just a general sense of happiness and joy.

I don't recommend continuing after 14 days, because then it may become a chore and not have the impact we are looking for. Can you do this again a few months down the road, or maybe next year? ABSOLUTELY! You can truly never encourage someone too much!

Choosing to let your spouse know not to expect any more notes is an individual choice, but an ideal time for a date night to discuss the impact that this has had on your relationship (from both sides). If you have children, this can also be a great conversation on how to use this to encourage them!

CHAPTER 8

Samples for Women to use with their spouse or significant other

If you are married:

1. Honey, there is no doubt in my mind that I love you more today than when we got married.

2. Honey, thank you for working every day at your job to provide for our family. I know it is hard, and you are amazing!

3. I love waking up next to you in the morning. It causes me to smile and thank God for you in my life.

4. I pray for our marriage every morning when I wake up, as I never want anything to come between us.

5. You have the biggest heart I know of any man for his family, thank you!

If you are with a significant other:

1. I can't wait for the day we can become husband and wife.

2. Meeting you has been a blessing from God for me, thanks for coming into my life.

3. Did you ever think we could be so happy together? This is amazing!

4. Doing life with you is such fun, you are such a giving person, and I am learning so much!

Get creative, get playful!

If you love seeing your husband in the shower, let him know that. You need to be his biggest fan, always!

CHAPTER 9

Pastor Message

If you use this book as a tool for your church, whether in a church-wide message or in a life or small group setting, here are notes to help you prepare. The following are some of the most important benefits of encouragement:

1. When we hear encouragement, we are able to draw upon an energy that enables us to accomplish things we may have thought impossible. An encouraging word works like an energy drink providing strength to overcome any obstacles that lay between us and our goal. Knowing there's someone out there cheering for us, might be all we need to cross the finish line.

2. Words of encouragement bring light to our dark world – the gift of hope. Hope motivates us to take one small step, then another, until we are back in the light.

3. Encouragement helps us to change our view on life. When we are in the middle of a storm, we can get lost and confused. We can perceive our circumstances differently. Stormy times can point our focus on petty things. A word of encouragement can help to calm us and make us stop to analyze what's going on in our life.

4. Encouragement is a great motivator. It helps to make people thrive. To thrive in anything we undertake on our own is hard. When someone encourages us, serves as our cheerleader, we become healthier in how we work.

If you're looking to facilitate an amazing shift in your church and/or group, I believe helping them understand the power of encouragement and its ripple effects will nudge that positive change along.

This book was written to help change a person's life and all those around them. If you do a sermon on this, I would love to know about any feedback you receive. If you use this in a group setting, please provide me stories of the impact you will see.

Q&A WITH THE AUTHOR

WHERE DID YOU FIRST GET THE IDEA FOR THIS SERIES?

I don't remember exactly how this idea came to me, it might have been around valentines day and I was trying to get creative with the men in my group on doing something special for their wives. They didn't want to write a love letter, so it began with taking a handful of Post It notes, writing mini love letters to their wives, and seeing what happened.

After doing this over many years, the process became refined and tested and successful based on numerous testimonies.

WHAT WAS THE BIGGEST CHALLENGE FOR YOU IN WRITING THIS BOOK?

The methodology isn't complex, but following the process is critical for a successful outcome. Writing that process out and detailing it with examples for all relationships was challenging, but then creating a study around it was a little more complex.

HOW DID YOU GET INTO WRITING?

All my life I felt this urge inside me to write a book. I had no idea about what, but felt there was this hole to fill.

And then it just came to me one day… change the world one relationship at a time!

WHO DO YOU MOST WISH WOULD READ YOUR BOOK?

If you have a relationship, especially married couples, this could rock your world. The beauty of this is that it can be applied to ANY relationship: your kids, your Church staff, the people you work with, your relatives… the list is endless!

www.ingramcontent.com/pod-product-compliance
Lightning Source LLC
Chambersburg PA
CBHW042047050426
42452CB00019BA/2965